I0410487

THE DEATH OF

INNOCENCE:

SURVIVING

TRAUMA

By

BOB FOLEY

© 2002 by Bob Foley. All rights reserved.

No part of this book may be reproduced, stored in a
retrieval system, or transmitted by any means,
electronic, mechanical, photocopying, recording, or
otherwise, without written permission from the author.

ISBN: 1-4033-5048-5 (e-book)
ISBN: 1-4033-5049-3 (Paperback)

This book is printed on acid free paper.

1stBooks – rev. 08/05/02

We owe it to those who didn't survive to teach others what we know, and to find some goodness, some meaning to this life.

From "Platoon"

Table of Contents

Chapter 1

The Problem

A nineteen-year-old Marine walking point down a jungle trail in a combat zone, a physically abused spouse arriving home from work, and a teenager coming home from school to an alcoholic parent; each is on a similar journey; each is a trauma survivor. As each enters his specific danger zone, the hyper-alertness of each sense is finely tuned. Each smell, sound or out of place sight may be a clue to what will happen next. Will s/he be safe entering this environment or is the wick already lit on an impending explosion?

We encounter trauma survivors every day. I've gotten so that I can recognize them by some behavior clues coupled with the depth of their eyes. In addition to the long-term trauma examples already given, they are victims of rape, gang rape, sex abuse, kidnapping,

1

murder and suicide witnesses, and survivors of incidents involving fatalities. The sense of powerlessness and the awareness of the possibility of having not survived, give young trauma victims the look of old souls in young bodies.

Survivors have a tendency to become over-involved in taking care of others, doing for others what they should be doing for themselves, but often at the same time experiencing a sense of detachment, an inability to feel really close to others.

I have known combat survivors who embarrassed themselves in displaying both a severe startle response and flashbacks while merely walking down the street. The backfire of a car engine sent one vet diving for the street gutter while another I knew whose job it was in Vietnam to drive a truck loaded with supplies, breaks into a cold sweat if he ever has to drive over something lying in the road. The memory of booby traps and land mines are quickly recalled when confronted with a pop can or paper bag in the road. It's no surprise that his favorite pastime now is to fly, where there's no worry at all about driving over anything.

Survivors often are excitement freaks, doing dangerous things to re-experience the adrenaline rush of the original trauma. This is often coupled with satisfying a sense of guilt for having survived, for having not been in as much danger as another was. Many survivors ride motorcycles or enjoy risky endeavors such as skydiving, bungee jumping or chemical use. Many choose occupations that either satisfy the need to help others or the danger aspect, or both, such as police officer, firefighter, private investigator, nurse (especially in the emergency room), paramedic, flight nurse, teachers, counselors, etc.

Many survivors are people-pleasers and perfectionists since self-worth is so integral to success for them. They become work-alcoholics and therefore are also able to avoid having to deal with very many, or very intense personal relationships. It gives them an out. They also have a deep sense of reality. They're often not idealistic at all and have lost any veneer of bravado or false bravery. They know what true fear is and how difficult it is to perform in the grips of fear. Even when they have performed well in extremely

3

fearful situations, the memory of the fear removes any sense of heroics.

It is difficult for survivors to trust others, since they have often experienced so many broken promises and so many situations where they didn't know what to expect. They're very self-reliant and often because of memory impairment issues do not trust themselves in social situations. As Mark Twain said, "It's better to be quiet and thought a fool than to open one's mouth and remove all doubt." Because of this, many survivors are very deep and introspective. One I know to this day is saddened by the memory of waiting all afternoon when he was about 8 to buy a pony, a promise made by an alcoholic father who instead spent the afternoon getting drunk and watching baseball on TV.

The survival techniques of a trauma sufferer are truly a natural reaction to an unnatural situation. There is a tendency to overreact to pressure from outside sources such as the everyday occurrences of traffic tie-ups or flat tires, but to under-react to anything that would normally cause a strong emotional response. A teenager I knew, Audrey had begun spending time with older acquaintances, one of whom was a Vietnam Vet. As one of Audrey's girlfriends began complaining about what a bad life she had and how she wanted to end it all, this vet calmly handed her a loaded gun and barely flinched as she stuck the barrel into her mouth and pulled the trigger. Audrey's premature encounter with her own mortality after witnessing her friend's death, left her with a mental picture she could never erase, and guilt for not being able to stop her.

Many young people experience such severe trauma so early in their lives that they somewhat experience their mid-life crisis as a teenager. The beginning of the movie, "Platoon", is a vivid example of this. During Vietnam, Army personnel did a twelve-month tour of duty in-country. As the Charlie Sheen character disembarks from the plane that brought him to Vietnam, he and his fellow "cherry" recruits pass a file of seasoned troops heading the opposite way, leaving Vietnam bound for "the World". The chronological difference in the two opposite-heading files is twelve months, but the demeanor and the look in the eyes of the two groups appear to be decades apart. In addition to having aged, the experienced group seems to have a truly discernible edge of sadness.

Survivors have lost their illusions of the world as it might have been and to protect themselves from any further pain, often psychologically numb their feelings, putting up walls so that nothing else will get through. In doing so, it is almost inevitable that destructive relationships reminiscent of the initial traumatic event will continue to occur until the feelings and issues are brought into the open and processed.

Many survivors have a difficult time developing and maintaining close personal relationships. This causes much stress within families where often the children of survivors feel there is a wall between them and their parent, and assume it is their fault. They often live their lives trying to figure out what they did wrong.

Often, the children of survivors take on the characteristics of survivors themselves! They repeat destructive relationships reminiscent of the relationship with the parent who is a survivor. The goal is to "fix" the other person in order to make up for the fact that s/he was not able to "fix" the survivor parent. Obviously, this attempt is doomed to failure, which increases the need to find someone to fix, so the cycle continuously repeats itself.

The most common example I have found of this cyclical relationship is the female child of a male alcoholic. Quite often she will choose male partners who have many of the negative characteristics of her father, and continue to stay with them no matter how bad it gets. Even if she is able to get out of one of these relationships, she almost invariably gets into another relationship with similar characteristics. The goal seems to be to stay with him, no matter what, and through the power of her love, change him. It just does not work.

There is a strong sense of emptiness that often leads to inappropriate bonding, arrested individuation and a lack of boundaries. Life becomes a problem to be solved involving the tolerance of the intolerable and acceptance of the unacceptable interspersed with periods of no tolerance at all. The repression of feelings is the major problem and the goal in recovery is to make the covert, overt, rather than the destructive process of re-creating the traumatic experience to try to master it. Co-Dependency is when the survivor thinks she caused something outside herself, but is convinced she can control it, and eventually cure it. She often lives in a gray world, reacting as if it were black and white.

Bonnie was a sixteen-year-old who was in one of my support groups as a result of being sexually molested by her biological father. As she began to process what had happened to her and the feelings that had remained buried for years, she was also able to admit to having been sexually molested by a neighbor, to having molested her own younger brother and to having attempted suicide numerous times.

Carol was a seventeen-year-old who moved out of state to get away from a father who had sexually abused her and a brother who had shot her. In my group, she was also processing her molestation by an uncle, sexual acting out to the point of suffering from sexually transmitted diseases, and a history of failed suicide attempts. She came to me one day with an audiotape she found in her locker in which her boyfriend said that by the time she played the tape, he would have killed himself by driving his truck into a bridge. As Carol, her boyfriend's father, a police officer and I waited in my office for word of the errant boyfriend, word came over the police officer's radio that the truck had been found. The driver had unfastened his seat belt so that when he hit a bridge abutment, he would be propelled through the windshield. Miraculously, he survived.

No matter what incident precipitated the traumatic response, survivors have six major issues that must be processed in order to move on in their lives. These are anger, guilt, loss, control, vulnerability and purpose.

Chapter 2

Anger

Anger is the strongest and most visible response to trauma. It is anger often born of powerlessness. The physically abused, the raped, and the survivors of combat situations often react violently when confronted by situations reminiscent of a traumatic event in which survival was not within their control.

Dave was a Vietnam Vet who was the sole survivor of his unit when they were overrun by a unit of the North Vietnamese Army. He survived by hiding behind the blade of a tractor and feigning death. An enemy soldier even nudged him with his rifle, but the hoax was successful. Decades later a young punk made the mistake of pulling a knife on Dave and demanding his wallet. The anger exploded and Dave's fist flew through the air with such velocity that the would-be robber's tooth was embedded in Dave's hand and surgery was required.

The anger may be directed at God, at others, or inwardly at the survivor himself. In addition to powerlessness, there are usually also feelings of frustration and abandonment, with an additional sense of impotence. Those who try to keep the anger inside tear themselves up emotionally similar to what a bullet shot into a military tank does; it just keeps bouncing around wounding more than one person until it is totally absorbed. Once the true source of the anger is realized, it can be processed and awareness can be developed so that the anger is noticed as it begins to develop. Strategies can be learned to process the anger before it gets to explosive stage. Deep controlled breathing, visualization, and some acceptable form of physical outlet can process the anger before it explodes. Walking, running, jumping rope, chopping wood, hitting a punching bag or a pillow are all ways to physically process the anger before it is a problem.

It seems to be especially necessary for the physical outlet component to take place, in particular to have some visual reminder that the anger has been released. The chopped wood is a good example of this, but if old, unused furniture can be available to be broken up or bricks can be smashed or even old, unused glasses or dishes can be broken, the release of the anger seems to be especially poignant. The expulsion of the energy, the visible clues that the energy has been expunged, and the release of endorphins all seem to work together to give the survivor relief.

The form of visualization I have found most successful involves deep controlled breathing, in through the nose and mouth, then slowly exhaling through the mouth only. At the same time, with the eyes closed, a safe, familiar place is visualized. The survivor is at first sitting in the shade in this environment, but the sun is visualized slowly moving up and warming each part of the body until a deep sense of warmth, relaxation and peace is realized.

If the anger is not appropriately processed, and in particular if young survivors are not given parental permission to express the anger appropriately, it is turned inward and can become depression and suicide.

It is amazing how often adolescents who are acting out, getting in trouble in school and with the police, getting in fights or refusing to perform at the level of ability where they could, are actually dealing with depression. Usually a combination of private counseling, group counseling and anti-depressant medication is what is needed.

Sometimes the remembered sense of powerlessness causes the survivor to identify with and take on the mannerisms of the perpetrator. There have been instances of prisoners of war taking on the attributes of their torturers, subconsciously hoping to take on some of their power in a way similar to what primitive tribes have done in taking scalps, using totems and practicing cannibalism.

Some survivors have a strong fear of allowing themselves to feel anger, especially those who have killed in wartime, since they know they have crossed the line, broken the taboo and taken a life. Even though it was justified at the time, the fear is that since it was done before, it could easily happen again. There is a tendency to overreact to things outside of the survivor, like a flat tire, but to under react to things inside, like the death of someone close. Creating chaos in his life often serves the dual purpose of helping a survivor feel truly alive and at the same time justify his rage reaction to the everyday problems of life. It can be helpful to be reminded that Blessed are the flexible, for they won't be bent out of shape!

The days hover like shadows about man. Each day, in which no good was done, returns to its Creator in disgrace.

Hillel Zeitlin

In the very depths of your soul, dig a grave; let it be as some forgotten spot to which no path leads; and there in the eternal silence bury the wrongs which you have suffered. Your heart will feel as if a load had fallen from it, and a divine peace come to abide with you.

Unknown

Happiness is not found, it is made. One can only give the seed of happiness to another. Each one must make it grow within himself.

Marciso Irala

A task without a vision is drudgery; a vision without a task is a dream; a task with a vision is victory.

Unknown

Maturing is the process by which the individual becomes conscious of the equal importance of each of his fellow (people).

Alvin H. Goeser

One of the most serious thoughts that life provokes is the reflection that we can never tell, at the time, whether a word, a look, a touch, an occurrence of any kind, is trivial or important.

E. V. Lucas

To hate another human being is to take a worm into one's own vitals. It consumes life.

Pearl S. Buck

God gave us a mouth that closes and ears that don't, which should tell us something.

C. W. Shedd

He who strikes the first blow has run out of ideas.

The Talmud

He who gains a victory over others is strong; but he who gains a victory over himself is all-powerful.

Lao-tse

Two things a person should not be angry at: what (s/he) can help and what (s/he) cannot help.

Unknown

Everybody thinks of changing humanity and nobody thinks of changing himself.

Leo Tolstoy

Whatever is begun in anger ends in shame.

Benjamin Franklin

S/He is a fool who cannot be angry; but s/he is wise who will not.

English Proverb

Anger is an acid that can do more harm to the vessel in which it's stored than to anything on which it's poured.

Unknown

Anger is a wind, which blows out the lamp of the mind.

Robert Ingersoll

He who cannot forgive breaks the bridge over which he himself must pass.

George Herbert

I have made a pilgrimage to Hiroshima. In the center of the city they have kept the ghostly, twisted ruins of the former exhibition hall and have made it a permanent exhibition of death, idiocy, and shame. A wire fence has been erected around the ruin. As it stands, it is to be the central memorial. On a standard outside, designating the mass of horror, is one word only, inscribed in large, bold letters. The word is **PEACE.**

Charles T. Leber

He who saves one life is considered as if he had preserved the whole world.

The Talmud

Chapter 3

Guilt

Self-talk creates the self-concept, both pictures and feelings that determine behavior and performance. The self-talk of a trauma survivor is that of guilt: guilt for what s/he did, guilt for what s/he should have done but didn't, or guilt for surviving when someone else didn't.

Ernie was a nineteen-year-old doing his tour of duty in Vietnam. Wartime is made up of long periods of boredom looking for something to do to fill up time, punctuated by short spasms of sheer terror. Ernie and his buddy decided to commandeer a jeep and head into Saigon to have some fun and drink some brew. After a night of celebration, along the road back to their firebase, the call of nature proved to be too much and Ernie pulled to the side of the road. Both soldiers jumped out of the jeep and headed for the nearest tree to relieve themselves. Ernie's ears seemed to explode and he was not able to make himself turn away from the shower of mutilated human body parts that rained down on him and the jeep as the booby-trapped tree his friend chose as a latrine exploded. Ernie was never able to completely let go of the guilt for stopping the jeep where he did, and for choosing the safe tree. This kind of guilt caused the deaths, by suicide and suspicious circumstances like single car accidents and motorcycles run into walls, of at least three times as many Vietnam Vets after the war as were lost during the war.

Guilt is especially prevalent among young sex abuse or molestation survivors. Adult perpetrators are especially adept at convincing victims that in some way, the incident or series of incidents were their fault. They dressed too provocatively, they were in a place where they shouldn't be, they didn't protest strongly enough, fight hard enough, run fast enough. Sometimes survivors are convinced by the perpetrator that deep down they really wanted the incident to happen. In particular, if there were any pleasurable

Bob Foley

feelings associated with the incident, any rewards such as gifts or special attention, even with all the guilt and pain and powerlessness, it is sometimes easy to convince young survivors that they were equal partners in what happened.

Kandi came to me as a ninth grader. She had a history of chemical use, trouble with the law, suicide attempts and a peer group of troublemakers. She was the youngest child in a large family, so when the acting-out behavior got to be too much for the parents to handle, she was sent to live with an older sister. Things seemed to be going pretty well, until she started visiting the nurse's office more and more often at school, primarily complaining of headaches.

She was referred to her counselor, but did not open up to any possible traumas from her past. She began to have some conflicts with peers, and in one instance the problems got to the point of a student threatening to beat Kandi up. This threat of violence towards her caused an emotional crisis and in pursuing the reason for the strong reaction to this threat, Kandi opened up about her past.

When she was 5 years old, Kandi and a friend of the same age were held at knifepoint by two teenaged boys and raped. The rape also involved one of the boys inserting the knife into the vagina of the other girl, which caused additional bleeding. The boys' stepfather observed the whole process. Since the community in which they lived was a very small community with the residents almost universally members of the same religion, of which the step-father was a respected leader, the boys were only held by the police for two days, then released. The girls received some counseling, then the incident was pretty much just hushed up.

When Kandi was in the 9th grade, her behavior started changing and she started to act out and get into trouble. During an experiment in science class that involved using a knife, she suddenly became extremely distraught and cut both wrists. Because of some comments related to the incident when she was 5 that Kandi had made, she was even confronted by members of her church, and questioned as to whether or not she were "unclean". She had to deal with one of the highest levels of guilt I had ever seen. She carried with her, from an early age, the "damaged goods" syndrome common to those who have been sexually abused.

I have known young people who were so angry with a parent that they wished them dead, only to have it actually happen. One such youth was convinced she had the power to cause another's death any time she chose, as a result of such an incident. Survivors need to learn that nothing they could have done or not do would justify the abuse they experienced.

The Vietnam Memorial in Washington D.C. is the most solemn, moving, oft-visited sight one could experience. It's starkness, solemnity, and graphic display of the over 58,000 lives lost in that war often evokes long-buried feelings related to that most difficult time in our history.

Greg was a helicopter door gunner during his tour of Vietnam. Helicopters often flew missions in support of ground operations. Greg had never talked about any of the operations in which he was involved and on a trip to "The Wall" with a group of other Vietnam Vets to celebrate the tenth anniversary of that monument, it became apparent why. In deep emotional sobs, Greg told of an operation involving air cover for advancing ground troops. A smoke screen was also employed and the ground troops were told to stay behind the smoke screen, that everything in front of the screen was considered enemy and thus targets for the door gunners.

Greg's machine gun was shooting almost incessantly as numerous enemy targets presented themselves. Suddenly he felt a sharp rapping on the top of his helmet and the screamed orders, "Stop Firing! Stop Firing!" Some of the American troops had carelessly wandered past the smoke screen and had thus become targets for Greg's blazing machine gun. It is difficult enough to deal with taking the life of another, even during wartime and in self-defense. But to know that you erroneously took the life of a comrade in battle is extremely difficult. The guilt can be almost insurmountable. Greg's guilt was self-inflicted, and one of the consequences of this continual guilt-related stress was a heart attack at a very early age.

In dealing with guilt, I try to get my survivors to picture guilt as a load of bricks sitting on a table, while each survivor wears an empty backpack. Many people will try to get survivors to pick up some of those bricks to put them in their backpack. Sometimes it's perpetrators, sometimes police, church officials, school officials, parents, siblings, and counselors, sometimes even fellow survivors who do not want to shoulder their burden alone. No matter which of the three types of guilt mentioned is an issue, the only one who can put a brick in the backpack is the survivor him/herself. Survivors have the choice of either being proud of having survived, or ashamed.

Probably the most difficult of the types of guilt to understand is the survivor guilt. Why should one feel guilty for surviving a situation that could have killed him/her, but didn't, but did take another life? There is a dichotomy in the thought process of a survivor in which the message is "I'm so sorry you didn't survive. I'd give anything to take your place in Death so you could be the one to survive, but Thank God I survived."

The young man who has not wept is a savage, and the old man who will not laugh is a fool.

George Santayana

Happiness is not so much in having as sharing. We make a living by what we get, but we make a life by what we give.

Norman MacEwan

Obstacles are those frightful things you see when you take your eyes off the goal.

Hannah More

Experience is a good school, but the fees are high

Heinrich Heine

Character isn't built on ease, success, a million dollars or a happy life. Mainly through pain, sorrow and adversity are the bricks fashioned, which can erect an enduring edifice.

Faith Baldwin

The conditions of conquest are always easy. We have but to toil awhile, endure awhile, believe always, and never turn back.

William Gilmore Simms

Free will and determinism, I was told, are like a game of cards. The hand that is dealt you represents determinism. The way you play your hand represents free will.

Norman Cousins

We seem to spend our lives making mistakes, which we spend our lives trying to make up for.

Harold Robbins

Two men look out through the same bars: One sees the mud and one the stars.

Frederick Langbridge

A person, like the bridge, was designed to carry the load of the moment, not the combined weight of a year at once.

William A. Ward

God has put something noble and good into every heart, which His hand created.

Mark Twain

Many people go throughout life committing partial suicide – destroying their talents, energies, creative qualities. Indeed, to learn how to be good to oneself is often more difficult than to learn how to be good to others.

Joshua Loth Liebman

You cannot do a kindness too soon, because you never know how soon it will be too late.

Unknown

If I were a godfather wishing a gift on a child, it would be that he should always be more interested in other people than in himself. That's a real gift.

Sir Compton MacKenzie

Peace is a value which man has always sought. Peace among nations, peace among men, but most of all peace of mind. While man has sought peace external to himself, he may have overlooked the fact that the peace that will influence all living things will be the peace that is first discovered within himself.

Cecil A. Poole

We live in the present, we dream of the future, but we learn eternal truths from the past.

Mme. Chiang Kai-Shek

I will not permit any person to narrow and degrade my soul by making me hate him.

Booker T. Washington

Life is mostly froth and bubble,

Two things stand like stone –

Kindness in another's trouble,

Courage in your own.

Adam Lindsay Gordon

How poor are they who have not patience!

What wound did ever heal, but by degrees?

William Shakespeare

Chapter 4

Loss

The loss issue is extremely prevalent among adolescent survivors. The loss may be of an actual person through death, geographical relocation or divorce; of a relationship; or of a part of the survivor him/herself, such as his/her innocence or ability to enjoy life in any way. The deep sense of loss must be expressed and the process of mourning followed: denial, anger, bargaining, depression, and finally acceptance.

Frank was a thirteen-year-old who was sent by his mom to live with his terminally ill father until the death occurred, so Frank would have memories of who his dad was. Frank attended school and developed relationships with fellow students as well as an older neighbor who befriended him. The day after his dad's death, before the funeral and without an opportunity to say good-bye to any of his new friends, Frank was uprooted and sent back to mom. His multiple loss issues took much time to process. Rituals such as funerals are very important to survivors because they function to reestablish a sense of belonging, a sense of meaning and a future orientation.

Many young people assume that when there is a loss in the family in some way it was their fault. Sometimes they think it is something they did and sometimes something they did not do that they should have. Some younger kids even see death as more of abandonment, that somehow the adult chose to leave, and this feeling gives rise to much anger.

When separation is not a result of death, the young person's behavior often changes in an attempt to get the lost adult back. Behavior can greatly improve in an attempt to woo the adult back by pleasing him/her. Sometimes the behavior greatly decreases in the hopes the adult will see the need to return to rectify the situation. Increased behavior problems in school and/or lower grades are often an attempt to send a message to a missing adult and/or to feel in control of some area in his/her life.

For the generation that fought in Vietnam, there is an extremely overwhelming sense of loss, which especially manifests itself at the Wall in Washington. There is an innocence, a hope for the future that for them died with John Kennedy and was buried in Vietnam. Having been raised in the fifties on a steady diet of John Wayne movies and having an idealistic picture of America at War, what happened in Vietnam came as a shock. Comparing WWII to Vietnam shows many differences. Instead of an average age of a combat solder of 27, in Vietnam it was 19. Instead of major combat operations followed by withdrawal to safe areas, there were no safe areas in Vietnam; it was hard to tell who your enemy was. Instead of a slow-moving troop ship bringing vets back home, allowing time to process many of the combat related issues, it was a matter of a series of airplane trips bringing troops home in less than 24 hours. It was not uncommon in Vietnam for a soldier to be pulled out at the end of a tenacious firefight, and sent back home so quickly that as he reached for a Pepsi at a local 7-11, noticed he still had blood under his fingernails from his last firefight.

One of the major issues adding to the trauma suffered by Vietnam Vets was their reception home. Instead of the warm reception and sense of welcome given to the WWII vets, the returning Vietnam Vet was vilified, spat upon, called "baby killer', ignored, feared, left unemployed, not trusted, and even looked down upon by the Veteran's Administration and Veteran Fraternal Organizations. This is similar to survivors of other traumas like rape and molestation being disbelieved, or even worse, blamed for what happened to them. There is a deep sense of loss for the way the world should be, for those in these types of situations.

Because of the sense of loss of a survivor, trust and a sense of idealism are often gone. The survivor must often learn to grant a guarded trust to others to find the happy medium between blind trust and total isolation. Not trusting is a way of not being hurt again, but it also prevents truly living life. Personal relationships often

Bob Foley

suffer when there is a fear of developing strong attachments.

The measure of a (person) is the way (s/he) bears up under misfortune.

Plutarch

To bear up under loss; to fight the bitterness of defeat and the weakness of grief; to be victor over anger, to smile when tears are close; to resist disease and evil men and base instincts; to hate hate, and to love love; to go on when it would seem good to die; to look up with unquenchable faith in something ever more about to be - that is what any (person) can do, and be great.

Zane Grey

A great (person) is (s/he) who has not lost the heart of a child.

Mencius

We cannot tell what may happen to us in the strange medley of life. But we can decide what happens in us – how we take it, what we do with it –

and that is what really counts in the end. How to take the raw stuff of life and make it a thing of worth and beauty – that is the test of living.

Joseph Fort Newton

They say to fruit-bearing trees: "Why do you not make any noise?" The trees reply: "Our fruits are sufficient advertisement for us."

The Midrash

To live in the hearts we leave behind is not to die.

Harold Robbins

Reflect upon your present blessings, of which every (person) has many; not on your past misfortunes, of which all have some.

Charles Dickens

Use what talents you possess: the woods would be very silent if no birds sang there except those that sang best.

Henry Van Dyke

Every human being is intended to have a character of his own; to be what no other is, and to do what no other can do.

William Ellery Channing

Perhaps parents would enjoy their children more if they stopped to realize that the film of childhood can never be run through for a second showing.

Evelyn Nown

The real object of education is to give children resources that will endure as long as life endures; habits that time will ameliorate, not destroy; occupations that will render sickness tolerable, solitude pleasant, age venerable, life more dignified and useful, and death less terrible.

Sydney Smith

Who takes vengeance or bears a grudge acts like one whom, having cut one hand while handling a knife, avenges him by stabbing the other hand.

The Jerusalem Talmud

Beauty is something wonderful and strange that the artist fashions out of the chaos of the world in the torment of his soul

W. Somerset Maugham

Character is the sum of all we struggle against.

Booker T. Washington

Who has never tasted what is bitter does not know what is sweet.

German Proverb

Your pain is the breaking of the shell that encloses your understanding.

Kahlil Gibran

It is by those who have suffered that the world has been advanced.

Leo Tolstoy

There are no hopeless situations; there are only people who have grown hopeless about them.

Clare Booth Luce

Chapter 5

Control

The traumatic event gave many survivors a deep sense of not being in control of their lives. A rape victim often felt totally powerless as the assault was perpetrated. The indelible memory of this powerlessness, until it is recognized and dealt with, can effect the survivor's life drastically.

The sense of powerlessness gives rise to a search for something in the survivor's life that will give her a sense of control. Young people who have the ability to do well in school but sabotage every effort to help them are often unidentified survivors. Greta was a pretty ninth grader who started getting in trouble with chemicals, her grades in school began to drop drastically, and she began to dress in a sensual manner. She finally came to me to admit what I had sensed: she was a survivor who had been molested as a five year old by a brother's friend, and was gang raped at the age of eleven. Her search for a sense of control caused her to sabotage school grades, dress in a manner that would cause her to feel some power over males along with the excitement of flirting with danger, and to extend the flirting with danger to using chemicals that were also a search to self medicate her emotional pain. Other survivors search for control by involvement in the various eating disorders, difficulties with the law, and the ultimate sense of control: suicide.

Sometimes this quest for control manifests itself in a hypersensitivity to injustice. There is such a deep sense of offended justice due to whatever the trauma was, that any reminder of that injustice elicits a strong emotional reaction. Students who are survivors will often react strongly to a teacher whom they perceive as treating anyone unfairly and will often be out-spoken champions of issues of fairness. Survivors learn at an early age that adults in their lives only have the control over them that the survivor gives them. They therefore often do not respond to the consequences that will often change other young people's behavior.

Grounding and removal of privileges are often seen by survivors as a small price to pay to feel in control.

While young survivors often try to find their sense of control related to school in some way, adult survivors often seek control through their families. Adult survivors find it most difficult to separate from their significant others and/or their children. They often allow themselves to become over-involved in these other people's lives, frequently doing for them what they should be doing for themselves. As a result of this over involvement, the survivor expects a high degree of loyalty from those in whom so much has been invested. When children enter adolescence and start their needed rebellion, this is often seen as inappropriate disloyalty by the adult survivor and is often met by increased restrictions, emotional distancing, and an attempt to "quash the rebellion."

This is dealt with in the family often following a pattern related to birth order. The oldest child, the hero, may cut the rebellion short and renew efforts to do well in every activity attempted. If that sibling can achieve well enough, it's a message to the world that the family is really o.k. The middle child is the rebellion leader and rebels in very outward, easily detectable forms. This scapegoat is the identified problem in the family upon whom everyone can concentrate their efforts to try and "fix" this family. The youngest is the lost child who withdraws from all the problems and lives in a fantasy world. There is rebellion here too, but it is more clandestine and not as easily detected. It doesn't matter if s/he doesn't get caught. Self-knowledge that the rebellion took place is enough. If there are 5 or more years between any of the siblings, s/he is treated like another oldest child. For survivors and their offspring, self-esteem is invested in a sense of control, either of themselves or of their family. It has even been found that strong behavior events that happen to one family member can be measured by stress level tests in the blood streams of other family members. Survivors show severe symptoms of chronic stress.

When control is found in no other way, and suicide is seen as the only alternative, it is important to be able to assess the degree of intent of the suicidal thought.

The SLAP method works well. How *S*pecific are the details, how *L*ethal the proposed method, how *A*vailable would the means be, and what is the *P*roximity of the means.

Life is like a camel. You can make it do anything except back up.

Marcelene Cox

The clock of life is wound but once,

And no man has the power

To Tell just when the hands will stop –

At late or early hour.

Now is the only time you own:

Live, Love, work with a will.

Place no faith in tomorrow, for –

The clock may then be still.

George H. Candler

Success is getting what you want;

Happiness is wanting what you get.

Unknown

(S/he) only is advancing in life whose heart is getting softer, whose blood warmer, whose brain quicker, whose spirit is entering into living peace.

John Ruskin

All that we are is the result of what we have thought. The mind is everything, What we think, we become.

Buddha

The story was told that near the end of the Vietnam War, a pilot who had often bombed a particular village was ordered to do so again. Knowing that little would be accomplished by doing so, and likening himself to a God holding the lives of the villagers in his hands, he magnanimously chose to drop his napalm into the neighboring fields rather than the village. Later, he had occasion to visit "his" village, the return of the savior. The first thing he noticed was a universal sense of depression; the second thing was a total absence of children. He stopped a passer-by to ask why. "During the whole war, we had been able to save our children by placing them in the safest place we knew. For some unknown reason, on the last air raid of the war, the napalm was dropped not on the village, the usual target, but on the children's safe haven, the neighboring fields."

Unknown

Parents owe it to the children they bring into the world to put the tools of living in their hands – hands which we have made as strong and capable as we can. But, having given them the hands and the tools, we owe it to them not to do their digging for them.

Lenora Mattingly Weber

The real solution of every problem can be found by those people who are hurt by it, if they will take hold of life where it hurts, and find out, not how they themselves can escape from that hurt, but how they can prevent that hurt from becoming a permanent factor in the lives of their brothers and sisters.

A. Mande Royden

LETTING GO

To let go doesn't mean to stop caring,

It means I can't do it for someone else.

To let go is not to cut myself off,

It's the realization that I can't control another.

To let go is not to enable,

But to allow learning from natural consequences.

To let go is to admit powerlessness,

Which means the outcome is not in my hands.

To let go is not to try to change or blame another;

I can only change myself

To let go is not to care for,

But to care about.

To let go is not to fix,

But to be supportive.

To let go is not to judge,

But to allow another to be a human being.

To let go is not to be in the middle

Arranging all the outcomes,

But to allow others to effect their own outcomes.

To let go is not to be protective;

It is to permit another to face reality.

To let go is not to deny

But to accept.

To let go is not to nag, scold or argue,

But to search out my own shortcomings and to correct

them

To let go is not to adjust everything to my desires,

But to take each day as it comes.

To let go is not to criticize and regulate anyone

But to try to become the dream I can be.

To let go is not to regret the past

But to grow and live for the future.

To let go is to fear less and love more

Fr. Robert Gehring

Chapter 6

Vulnerability

Most young people have a sense of being immortal and invulnerable. That is sometimes why they take part in risk-taking behavior such as driving fast, driving drunk, cliff diving, bungee jumping, etc. Trauma survivors have learned from life's experiences that this is not the case, that terrible things can happen to them or people they know. Many survivors picture themselves going through life with a target painted on their backs. Once a traumatic event has occurred, it is assumed many more are to come.

Harry was a high school senior who had been kidnapped at gunpoint. While he and a friend were sitting in his car in a bowling alley parking lot, two assailants with drawn guns came up to the open windows, forced the two boys into the back seat, and drove off into the back streets of the neighborhood. By luck, as the car turned onto the dirt road alongside a canal, the headlights silhouetted a parked police car. Harry and his friend took the opportunity to jump through the still-open windows and ran towards the police car, averting their own possible deaths.

For a long time after this event, Harry would become very uncomfortable in parking lots. Some survivors, more than expecting further trauma, almost feel they deserve more traumas in their lives. These feelings of vulnerability must be processed so that the survivor does not live a life of isolation, and yet realistic dangers must be acknowledged.

Some young survivors are easily picked on by other students, while other survivors are the ones who do the bullying, venting their anger and seeking to control others. Those who easily become targets are living their guilt and shame and expecting to pay for whatever it is they did or did not do. They almost always seem to have someone threatening to beat them up, spreading rumors about them, putting them down about something.

I try to get these young people to picture themselves living in a plastic dome at the bottom of "shit hill". It doesn't matter what people say, or in what way they throw shit down the hill, the self-constructed dome can be a protection. It can repel what you do not want to deal with, if you will only picture yourself using it.

Young survivors, or the children of survivors, learn at an early age that what happens to us in life is not totally dependent on the choices we make. There are many other factors out there that can determine whether or not we survive. For them, life is much like driving a car. There are many things you can do to make yourself safer; using a seat belt, never speeding, never driving under the influence, signaling every turn or lane change, etc. But they realize that nothing can be done to guarantee their safety. No matter how careful they are or how closely they follow the rules, something beyond their control can happen. A drunk driver can swerve into their path, someone can run a red light, and someone can cut in front of them without warning. Anything could happen without warning.

They have learned young that being alive is being vulnerable. The key is to keep the sense of vulnerability within limits that will allow everyday human functioning in society.

Time is a dressmaker specializing in alterations.

Faith Baldwin

Our days are like identical suitcases; all the same size but some people can pack more into them than others.

P. L. Andar

The grand essentials to happiness in this life are something to do, something to love, and something to hope for.

Joseph Addison

Happiness is not a station you arrive at, but a manner of traveling.

Margaret Lee Runbeck

Experience is not what happens to a (person). It is what a (person) does with what happens to (him/her)

Alduous Huxley

The world is what we think it is. If we can change our thoughts, we can change the world. And that is our hope.

H.M. Tomlinson

I am more and more convinced that our happiness or unhappiness depends far more on the way we meet the events of life than on the nature of those events themselves.

Wilhelm Von Humboldt

Let me do the thing that ought to be done, when it ought to be done, as it ought to be done, whether I like to do it or not.

Unknown

Our most severe challenges will one day reveal themselves to be our greatest teachers.

Betty J. Eadie

Our main business is not to see what lies dimly at a distance but to do what lies clearly at hand.

Thomas Carlyle

Every individual has a place to fill in the world, and is important, in some respect, whether he chooses to be so or not.

Nathaniel Hawthorne

We have a bat's eyes for our own faults, and an eagle's for the faults of others.

J. L. Gordon

The world is now too dangerous for anything but the truth, too small for anything but brotherhood.

A. Powell Davies

If we could read the secret history of our enemies we should find in each man's life sorrow and suffering enough to disarm all hostility.

Henry Wadsworth Longfellow

The wise man reads both books and life itself.

Lin Yutang

There are obviously two educations. One should teach us how to make a living, and the other how to live.

James Truslow Adams

Behold the turtle: He makes progress only when he sticks his neck out.

James Bryant Conant

Freedom and responsibility are like Siamese Twins: they die if they are parted.

Lillian Smith

The owl is therefore the bird of wisdom, because even a fool can see when it is light, it is the wise person that can see when it is dark.

Iran N. Panin

A problem is an opportunity in work clothes.

Henry J. Kaiser, Jr.

Be not afraid of life. Believe that life is worth living and your belief will help create the fact.

William James

Don't wish to have more, do more with what you have.

Unknown

Chapter 7

Purpose

The culminating issue that a survivor must face is to find a purpose for the painful experiences s/he has endured. Once s/he has dealt with the other issues, all the pain and effort to survive are wasted if not put to a purpose. This is also called the "survivor mission."

The highest purpose is to use the lessons of an individual's life to make the lives of others better. Many trauma survivors become peaceful, open and warm people to whom it is easy for others to come with their problems and find an attentive, nonjudgmental ear. Many trauma survivors find their way into the helping professions.

The life of a survivor can be an example to others, a beacon to show the way when a trauma seems to indicate the end of any positivism in a life. Many survivors come to the conclusion that the only way to live life is as if each day is the last, but at the same time, as if it's the first day of a long life. The balance needed to live such a life leans heavily on the Golden Mean, the happy medium in most decisions, with a strong balance of mind, body, and spirit. Keeping the mind active through reading, continued education, or research is important. The body can be kept healthy by exercise and monitoring amount and what is eaten. There is much research available about how food effects us, especially food allergies, sugar, food coloring, irradiated food and missing nutrients like Zinc. Many have difficulty grasping the idea of spirit. It can be approached as whatever gives meaning and direction to your life, of a religious nature or in some service to mankind.

For those who have been through a trauma, there are three ways to live life afterwards: as a victim, as a rudderless boat bounced through life by experience, or as a survivor. A survivor makes her life's goal the pursuit of peace, justice, and beauty. It is important for young survivors to process their issues, but many do not have the family support or financial resources to seek specialized therapy through an agency, so it often falls to the school counselor with a 400+ caseload to facilitate the catharsis. Support groups that meet weekly with a composition of five to twelve students work best. Members may stay in groups as long as they want, but new members are only added at designated times.

There are only three guidelines for the operation of the group, which include confidentiality, no put-downs, and one speaker at a time. Members can dialogue, comment, and question each other, but an atmosphere of trust is essential for the cathartic process to take place. Each speaker volunteers. No one is ever forced to speak. Breaches of the guidelines must be dealt with by the group as soon as possible and to the total group's satisfaction. Discussing, validating, and processing the six previously discussed issues in the protected environment of the group are vital for the members to be able to move on in their lives. The goal is to make the covert, overt.

There are three things that we all have in common: each has a purpose, each has problems in this life and each must deal with his own death. This commonality with others is especially poignant for survivors. When they realize they are not alone and that they have common issues with others, it becomes easier to see their survivor mission.

The mistake some make in developing their survivor mission is to make happiness a goal. That is a mistake because we humans do a poor job of choosing what we think will bring happiness. The result is often the opposite, such as the choices of promiscuity, chemical use, or buying sprees that survivors often use in seeking happiness. If peace, especially internal peace, is the goal, we tend to make better choices and thus find happiness as a corollary.

For survivors, life is often like a journey down a road that has a stone barrier between the road and a beautiful, expansive field. Where we are is the road, the field is our survivor mission and the barrier is the trauma that both separates us from our purpose and draws us to it. Once we process that trauma and surmount it, the vast beauty of our purpose, our mission, awaits us. As Jean-Paul Sartre has said,

"…by projecting myself toward my ends, I preserve the past with me, and by action I decide its meaning."

Danny was the child of an alcoholic. Being an oldest child, he developed early a strong sense of responsibility and need to achieve. It was important to him to always get good grades in school, never get into trouble, and excel at sports. The alcoholic father was not really abusive; he was just seldom there. The family was poor since the income level was already low, and pushed even lower by the money spent on alcohol. Danny seldom brought friends home since he was embarrassed by the furnishings and never knew what to expect from his dad…how would he embarrass Danny this time?

After his dad's death from cirrhosis, Danny quit college and joined the service early in the Vietnam War. He was following his sense of duty instilled in him by a childhood full of John Wayne movies, embarrassment for his Dad, who had never served in the military even during WWII and a sense of completing a mission started by John Kennedy.

Danny did three tours of Vietnam on an aircraft carrier, first saying good-by to his fiancée, on the second tour leaving his pregnant wife, and on the third leaving his wife and 2 year old daughter. Each tour also involved less and less belief in the justice of America's involvement in Vietnam. He was discharged overseas during his third tour. His disenchantment with the war was made obvious by the rebellious length of his hair and the peace sign on his duffel bag, but this also ostracized him from the other vets making the return trip to the U.S. There was a real sense of isolation, as no one would talk to him or acknowledge him. A stewardess even dripped hot coffee on him, seemingly on purpose.

His reception stateside was not much better. He was ignored and ostracized by civilians because he had been in the military, and he was ostracized by other vets because he had turned against the war. There was a real sense of fitting in no where. That strong sense of needing to do "the right thing", following duty, and trusting authority figures was completely blown away. The anger towards war protestors and "hippies" gave way to envy that they could rebel and actually think for themselves in some cases, as long as they protested the war and not the warriors.

There was also guilt for having survived the war when so many others had not. An aircraft carrier is safer than walking jungle trails in a combat zone, but to some degree it is like sitting on a leaking gasoline can while someone throws lit matches at you. Most of the time the matches go out, but every once-in-a-while, there's an explosion. One such incident was the route to Danny's survivor mission. This is his story:

In January of '69 on the way to my second Vietnam tour on an aircraft carrier, the ship was going through what is called an Operational Readiness Inspection, designed to verify that the ship operated at a level of expertise required to enter a combat zone.

Fighter aircraft loaded with missiles and napalm were lashed to the flight deck in readiness for practice bombing runs. However, the chains holding one of the jets to the deck were in the wrong position. Because of this, the operator of the small cart used to start the jet engines had to pull up to the jet at an awkward angle.

He didn't notice that the exhaust of his cart was pointed at the nose of a missile hanging from the jet's wing. The missile fired across the flight deck and hit another jet, exploding its napalm bombs and spreading the burning napalm across the flight deck. It then became a chain reaction of missiles and bombs being exploded and holes blown in the flight deck. Some pilots were already in their planes and most of those burned to death or ejected out of their planes, a few landing in the ocean, but most landing in the midst of the fire.

This incident happened only moments before a scheduled general quarters drill, so most people were already at or near their battle stations. If it had happened at 3:00 a.m. most of the 6,000-man crew could have perished.

I was eating breakfast when the first explosion occurred. In the short time it took to get up and head towards the engine room, which was my battle station, the wounded were already being brought to sick bay. I'll never forget the sight of my footprints going through the blood of the wounded already thick on the deck.

My battle station in the engine room was many feet below water level. We started getting smoke into the engine room through our ventilation system, our only source of air. It is scary to know you have to go up through fire to get to a point where you could jump overboard if we had to abandon the engine room. It changes your life to think you'll die when you are 22, to never see my pregnant wife and the baby girl she carried. The fire raged for many hours, but was eventually extinguished. Almost four hundred men were wounded, primarily from terrible burns and shrapnel. Almost 40 were killed.

I'll never forget coming out of that deep engine room to see the radiant sun and deep blue ocean off of Hawaii that I thought I'd never see again. Then my eyes fell on the terrible destruction on the flight deck, the burned and partially burned jet carcasses, and the smells of the chemicals used to fight the fire mixed with burned fuel, napalm, and burned human flesh. It sears through your lungs to your brain and stays there forever. I peered through one of the holes blown into the flight deck which opened into a restroom. Parts of the men who had been in there still floated in the water used to fight the fires. When I found out the cause of all this destruction, I had a deep sense of anger and loss. The careless mistake of one person, doing something as trivial as attaching a hold-down chain to a jet, had caused all this death and destruction. I determined then that since I had survived, I would do something worthwhile with my life, something that would help young people see the importance of making responsible decisions and acting in responsible ways. Becoming an educator seemed to be the best route to this end.

Children of survivors are secondary survivors and can learn to use what happened to them. This is the story of Danny's daughter:

The Vietnam War was 4 years old when I was born. The birth of the war had caused a rebirth of the nation and a subsequent restructuring of beliefs and ideals. The reconstruction spanned my lifetime: the formation of my ideals was shaped by the reformation of national ideals.

For six years of the War my dad was in the Navy. He was fulfilling what he believed to be his duty. He was released when I was two years old. His experience shook the foundations of his belief, his faith, his hope. It is from him that I learned about Vietnam and War in general. We have traveled on different aspects of the same path: from innocence to maturity and from ignorance to exposure. If it were not for the strength of his spirit…

It wasn't until the early years of grade school that I began to become aware of the Vietnam War and its effect on my parents' lives. The first tangible imagery came to me among the safe cushions of my living room. The smell of Jiffy Pop popcorn filled the air, wafting through the whir of the 8 millimeter projector. My dad proudly presented his "Navy films" as a preview to reels of my parents' wedding and the my first series: my first bath, my first cereal, my first fart. Exotic images of foreign ports bounced across the screen. My dad had shot much of the footage from buses, and the effect was real enough to make me carsick. I was intrigued by the vibrating images, but I sensed that there was much more to the Vietnam War than home movies. I saw nothing in the footage that would have made my mom cry. I had heard them talking, the adults, about Vietnam and my mom was crying. I thought abut asking my dad what his films had to do with war, or what about it would have made my mom cry, but my brother started throwing popcorn kernels at me and I soon forgot.

In 6th grade I had to do a report and I chose as my subject the ship my dad had served on. Now I had the perfect opportunity to learn about the Vietnam War. My dad retrieved the enormous, blue, leather smelling book I had leafed through many times. It sat between the Bible and the big book of photographs called "Our Family Album". The book had photos of the ship and lots of pictures of young-looking boys in funny uniforms. I was awestruck by the size of the ship, and amazed that it carried planes on top. I gasped with excitement as my dad told the story of the explosion that destroyed half of the ship. The proof was right there in black, billowing smoke! The questions flowed from my mouth like seawater through a porthole. Was my dad scared? Did people get hurt? Did he ever get seasick? Did he ever shoot anybody? Did he see any sharks? My dad always answered my questions in his calm and calculating manner. The imagery that fueled my imagination just as quickly extinguished it as my dad began to speak. He explained with solemn emphasis that people, some he knew, died in that fire. I came to know that war meant killing and Vietnam was a successful prototype.

Although I was young, I had enough intuition to sense that as he spoke, his mind was far away. The retelling was always soft and distant with an end that snapped back into life with vehement parables against War.

The dam of my innocence had burst and a flood of curiosity welled up inside me. The more I learned, the less I understood. I had seen the pictures in the movies and TV of soldiers with guns and tanks. The confusion depicted in those moments, where all that could be heard was pop! Pop! Popping!, made me wonder how anyone could know what they were shooting at. I was mostly disturbed at the absurdity of it all. People were dying!

Around this time my brothers were getting into the cops and robbers/cowboys and Indians stage and requests for toy guns finally had to be appeased. The house rule was that the toys, even water guns, could never, ever be pointed directly at anyone. Never.

My dad taught at the junior high next to my elementary school, so my brothers and I would walk over to his room after school. He was using pictures for one of his writing units and I sifted through them inquisitively. The other side of war was revealed in black and white: a young girl, naked, running across a bridge with her arms outstretched; her face twisted with pain. A baby screaming in terror, seen only in silhouette through a wall of flames. How could people do this?

My interest now had gone beyond the war into the realm of human nature that allowed such horror. During this time, I discovered music and I raided my dad's record collection regularly. I would sit with the earphones pressed to my head for hours listening to the Beatles, Jesus Christ Superstar (my brothers and I were known to give performances) and Carole King. I came across a 45 that struck me, because I didn't understand the words: "Anybody here seen my old friend Abraham? Can you tell me where he's gone? He freed a lot of people but it seems the good die young. I just looked around and he's gone." I asked my dad what it meant, where did these people go? An explanation and history lesson ensued after which I knew, to my confusion, that people that try to stop war get killed too.

My swirling emotions overflowed one night in the same, cushiony living room that introduced me to the exotica of War. I saw a TV movie on the Kent State murders and became so hysterical that my parents became concerned. My innocence had been shot down, bombed by the airplane of reality. The realization of the scope of the injustice in the world washed over me: from the crucifixion of Jesus to the assassination of Martin Luther King Jr.; from the students at Kent State, to the idiocy of racism and, most importantly, to the innocent people that die on either side when there's a war. I had been betrayed, and my parents held me and let me cry. The shock I felt as my illusions were shattered must have emulated my father's destroyed idealism of duty as well as the nation's horror at the price of patriotism. Vietnam delivered two generations into a silent stupor of disillusionment.

As the waters of realization receded and started a pond of cynicism in my heart, my dad was slowly digesting the gristle of war that had lodged in his stomach. As he confronted and absorbed his personal experience in Vietnam, he turned his disappointment into action. The flicker of hope, faith, and belief began to glow. A wall in our house was turned into a monument of peace: a collage of photos and posters celebrating the ideals and prophets of peace. The wall was also a homage, remembering the many people who experienced the War and the ones who lost their lives: martyrs for peace. The wall was an extension of the parental teaching put forth in an attempt to ensure that my brothers and I would never have to experience the pain and suffering that comes with War.

My dad overcame the pain of betrayal that had silenced him for so long and spoke out against the abandonment of thousands of POW/MIA's in Vietnam. His pursuit took him to the highest levels of government where he confronted the officials with their neglect and corruption. His duty went unappreciated once again. The popular theories of conspiracy began to seem more accurate to my dad as his own experience parodied them. The betrayal he felt of personal ideals was being paralleled on a much larger scale.

I couldn't rely on my high school history courses to give me the information I sought, so I continued to use my dad as a resource. We contemplated conspiracy theories and the affects of Agent Orange at the dinner table and he introduced me to books like The Razor's Edge and A Farewell To Arms. I followed my dad's lead and turned my disillusionment into action, becoming an outspoken political advocate for issues pertinent to me at the time: rain forest aide, reproduction freedom, Amnesty International, the abolition of apartheid. Unfortunately, I was still speaking out against the travesties of war: those that had occurred in Vietnam and those perpetually occurring all around the world.

My dad continued his reconstruction and turned to a theory of personal contribution. Refusing to be squelched by the blasphemous power structure, he turned his life into an example of passive resistance. He became active in the Vietnam Veterans of America, he started a therapy group for children of Vietnam Vets, and he volunteered for the Color Guard. He shifted from teaching to counseling and he now works full time helping young people deal with their harsh experience of reality and betrayal. He strives to instill in them the spirit of peace: the only chance for an end to War.

I'm 30 now and still struggle with a sense of disenchantment. It has been over a quarter of a century since the Vietnam War and I'm surrounded by conflict, complacency, and violence. There have been wars in my lifetime, in fact, some continuing to rage at this moment.

My only consolation is in the motivation and spirit I possess, thanks to the influence of my dad. I work at a non-profit organization, attempting to improve human rights. I also work as a tutor at an elementary school, answering millions of questions with truth and compassion. I can only hope to plant in my students the spirit that has bloomed in me.

My dad has come to terms with his experience in Vietnam. He will never forget, for to overcome something you must never forget it, but he now exudes a calm aura: the result of a thirty-year lesson in humanity. He divulges more of his emotions now than he ever has and has found peace in the simple pleasures of life: grand daughters, collecting books, grand daughters, mornings of solitude at a coffee shop with a book, and grand daughters. He has created a "goodness and meaning in this life".

Recently I saw my dad perform with the Color Guard at an annual gathering called Nam Jam. The moment came for the national anthem and the old flood that burst with the pain of my first betrayal and disillusionment returned in the form of tears. The rowdy crowd became silent and still under the shadow of an enormous American Flag. A single trumpet and voice could be heard; every hand was poised on the heart. All eyes, some wet with tears, were raised in reverence. There on the stage, in his starched uniform and white gloves, was my dad. His gaze was strong as he raised the flag of the POW/MIA's. I saw perseverance, patriotism, faith, and hope embodied in his pillar-like form. I surveyed the crowd and found the same spirit in the weathered faces. In the midst of their pain, through all their struggles of disillusionment, betrayal, and neglect, they still believed and they still had hope.

The greatest achievement of the human spirit is to live up to one's opportunities and make the most of one's resources.

Vauvenargues

The purpose of life is not to be happy – but to matter, to be productive, to be useful, to have it make some difference that you lived at all.

Leo Rosten

Many persons have a wrong idea about what constitutes true happiness. It is not attained through self-gratification, but through fidelity to a worthy purpose.

Helen Keller

Life's greatest achievement is the continual remaking of yourself so that at last you know how to live.

Winfred Rhoades

He has achieved success who has lived well, laughed often, and loved much; who has gained the respect of the intelligent, the trust of the pure and the love of little children; who has left the world a better place than he found it, whether by an improved flower, a perfect poem or a rescued soul; who has never lacked appreciation of earth's beauty or failed to express it; who has looked for the best in others and given them the best he had; whose life was an inspiration; whose memory a benediction.

Bessie A. Stanley

For every hill I've had to climb,
> For every stone that bruised my feet,
For all the blood and sweat and grime,
> For blinding storms and burning heat,
My heart sings but a grateful song…
> These were the things that made me strong.

For all the heartaches and the tears,

    For all the anguish and all the pain,

For gloomy days and fruitless years,

    And for the hopes that lived in vain,

I do give thanks, for now I know

    These were the things that helped me grow!

Unknown

Man never knows precisely what is right

So, torn between a purpose and a doubt,

He first makes windows to let in the light,

And then hangs curtains to shut it out.

Unknown

If we are to have peace, we must serve each other. Only through service can we find our-selves. It is not that others need us, but that we need others.

Madam Rajkumair Amrit Kaur

Live every day as if it were your last. Do every job as if you were the boss. Drive as if all other vehicles were police cars. Treat everybody else as if he were you.

Unknown

The difficult is just which can be done immediately; the impossible takes a little longer.

George Santayana

The only failure a person ought to fear is failure in cleaving to the purpose he sees best.

George Eliot

Every tomorrow has two handles. We can take hold of it by the handle of anxiety or the handle of faith.

Unknown

God gives every bird its food, but He does not throw it into the nest.

Josiah Gilbert Holland

A person has made at least a start on discovering the meaning of human life when s/he plants shade trees under which s/he knows full well s/he will never sit.

Elton Trueblood

Chapter 8

The Solution

Laura's story came out after a number of sessions in a support group. Her catharsis came through writing.

I am sixteen years old. My entire teenage life has been lived in fear. When I was thirteen, I remembered something that happened to me in my child hood. My biological father took something away from me that I will never be able to obtain again because with this you only have one chance. I lost my innocence when I was only three.

When I was eight years old my parents got a divorce and my biological father was put into prison for the molestation of my older sister. I can remember having to live in a one-bedroom apartment with my mother and my two siblings, it was so crowded. I had to live with my grandparents for almost a year and that disrupted my life due to the fact that I was going into the third grade and would have to be at a different school. My grandparents and my family got along okay but I especially became very close to my grandmother.

When summer after my third grade year came, my mother remarried. The new family consisting of my mother, stepfather, sister, brother, and myself, relocated to a slum neighborhood in California. My grandmother died when I was in the sixth grade and I was having a very difficult time becoming close to anyone, so one year when I went to a church summer camp after sixth grade, I met Fred.

After years of friendship, he asked me to go to his Winter Formal at his school so I got all dressed up in a gorgeous dress and my family carted me off on the twenty-mile drive to his house. I met his family and our parents talked. I would be staying in the guest room that night and going home the following day. The dance was great, I hadn't felt so close to anyone for so long, but that night brought back a terrible memory, one that I cannot clear from my head now, the memory of my father taking me into his bedroom and touching me all over. I didn't know what I was thinking or why this picture had come to me, but it did. After the dance, Fred's mom picked us up and we went back to his house. We spent almost the entire night together in the guestroom, me telling him what I had remembered and him crying and me crying. I didn't think that I could deal with it on my own and I was going to be moving later that month, 500 miles away from him. I didn't know what I was going to do, all I knew was that my biological father was long gone and he had gotten away with hurting me. I had had so many chances to remember this before when someone could have done something to help me. I couldn't understand why I didn't remember then.

Junior year brought a lot of heartache. In September, while my parents were off on business, our family home burned to the ground thanks to a leak in our propane tank. We had to relocate while they rebuilt our home and it was hard to go to school knowing that the life we had established was gone. By my sixteenth birthday we were back in the house and things for me just started getting worse and worse. I was in a support group through my school to deal with the feelings I was having about the childhood experience. I tried to commit suicide by taking half a bottle of ibuprofen, but it didn't work, I just got sick. In my support group my counselor made me tell my dad about the attempt and when I did he promised that he would help me get professional help. My junior year ended and summer started. This summer has been the worst ever. I didn't get help and I have tried to kill myself two times. I just want things to end for me; right now the way I am feeling is like nothing is ever going to be enough to fill the hole in my chest that should be my heart. I have to face the fact that I am going to graduate this year and that I will have to do something with my "life" after I do graduate. Life as I know it ended when I remembered my molestation, and I don't want to remember any more.

I am an outcast. Most of the people at my school hate me for no reason. They only hear gossip and what is upsetting is that they believe it. I only have three friends that are female and one male friend, but it feels almost like I have nobody. I don't want to trust anyone, but I need to have somebody. I really want to go back to California and forget what happened to me. While these people shouldn't matter to me, they do and I live in fear every day that somebody is going to come after me. I can't hide from the feeling if impending doom. I even have trouble sleeping and I can't stand feeling like I am not safe anywhere. I don't know how to change people but if I don't let people know who I really am then they are just going to draw their own conclusions and hurt me for what they think I am. I have been called various times a whore, slut, ho, dyke, weirdo, she-devil, and death itself. I have tried to explain to my parents why I need to be at a different school but I can't bring myself to tell them what people have said about me. I can't defend myself to the large amount of them. I am only one person who they see as a weak spot and they know that if they push the right buttons I will break. I have lost all self-control and it will be very hard to get back. I only know that who I think I am is not a bad person but someone who lets bad things happen to her. I feel that in some ways I deserve all of the hatred because I myself want to hate every person alive, but at least I have the morality to give them a chance. How can people be so mean and unhumanlike? What right do they have to pass judgement on someone they don't even know? I cannot find the answers to these and many other questions. All I know is that I am very vulnerable and weak. I don't want to let anyone into my head because it seems that no matter what I do I always end up hurt.

I am so empty inside that I would do almost anything to get that emptiness filled up. I have tried relationship after relationship and the hole hasn't been filled. I get all of the attention that I possibly can but that doesn't work either. I wish that I could find something that will fill this emptiness that I am feeling. I know that my family cares about me and I know that there are a lot of people who are willing to do everything within their power to help me when I am in a bad state of mind. I just can't seem to understand what it is that is wrong with me. There are no nights when I don't cry, no nights when I don't toss and turn and wake up a lot. My daily life has deteriorated because I don't like to go out anymore in fear that no one will want me to go out with them. The emptiness has taken over my entire heart and soul. I do not want to go on like this anymore, I figure that if I am so empty now it can only get worse and worse for me as I continue to grow up.

So many things have happened to me that are so bad that I feel that no matter what I do I will always fail. I have a hard time accepting any good things that are thrown my way and due to that not many good things do come. Sometimes I catch the good but I use it all up at once and then it is gone, forever. I don't know how to handle myself around anything good for a long time so I usually trash whatever that good is and then dump it so I don't have to deal with it anymore. (Laura dealt with all of these issues in group throughout her senior year.)

Life can be pictured as an ever widening, upward moving spiral. This accounts for our ever-widening circle of experience, our progression through our allotted time in this existence, and the cyclical nature of our lives, that some of our experiences tend to repeat until we learn the lesson we are meant to learn.

In this spiral journey through life, in time we learn the three major don'ts: don't ask <u>why</u>, don't say <u>can't</u>, and don't <u>should</u> upon yourself, putting yourself down for what you should be doing, should have done, should know, should have as a career, should have as an income, should anything. What is, is.

The survivor has arrived when s/he is able to love unconditionally, both himself and others, to let go of the need to be in total control of himself and /or others, and to be able to be a support for the others in her life without putting expectations on them. Life is precious and meant to be lived to the fullest. Morally each of us has within us the ability to be a saint, a sinner, and a human. We must remember being human is not being a sinner, and it's seldom that we'll be a saint. Healing is a process…recovery is a choice. All true effort to help others begins with self-humiliation – the helper must first humble himself under him he would help, and must understand that to help does not mean to be a sovereign, but to be a servant, that to help does not mean to be ambitious, but to be patient, that to help means to endure the accusation of being in the wrong and not understanding what the other understands. Learn from the other what s/he understands, in the way s/he understands it.

Some traumas are buried so deeply that survivors actually suffer from alexithymia – the inability to verbally articulate with true emotions their inner states and feelings. Feelings are then communicated through action-anger, and acting out. Creative arts therapies – dance, music, art, writing, drama, etc. can be a route to process the blocked feelings, to deal with the trauma without being overwhelmed. Art therapy in particular has been found to reduce the frequency and intensity of trauma-induced nightmares.

The kids of strictly religious parents sometimes exhibit mannerisms similar to children of alcoholics: they become sensation seekers to the point of being adrenaline junkies. It is important to be gently confrontive to help elicit the retelling, which is part of the healing. It helps to anchor strong emotions in different body parts, then that emotion can be recalled simply by touching that body part. Visualization of actions not taken in the past can create new mental pathways leading to positive behavior changes and a sense of empowerment for the future. Dealing with the issues related to trauma are less looking for a cure and more seeking manageability. Recovery is progress, not perfection. An activity that often helps with the healing is to write down what a survivor would want someone who harmed them to say. It can be as good as the person actually saying these things. It can allow the needed catharsis.

This Memorial Day

By Steve Mason

Every artist knows

That he must stretch his own canvas first,

That he become his own first work of art,

Then, and only then,

Can he or she interpret our world for us

It is the tautness of the inner-self

Which best reflects the brightness of being.

True art is a portrait of the artist's soul

It is in that which we find beauty

Each man knows

That the real journey is *within*

That he must know himself

Separate from all others.

He must have either a dream or a plan

Which defines him and is signatory

To his commitment of the time remaining him.

It is *his* life which he must experience.

In this he is a genius

(genius knows *without* learning).

Such a man, other men follow.

And in so doing, find themselves.

The Death of Innocence: Surviving Trauma

Every true artist is irreverent

(without *new* perspective there is only still life).

Each true man must be independent,

Trusting in his own judgment,

Willing to err on the side of action

(without passionate self-confidence

there is only "man-made"; unnatural, indeed).

They sing no ballads, nor write no poems

For bureaucrats;

Young boys do not posture

In the "water-cooler" stance

Or practice the listing shuffle

Of career office workers

Who seek promotion by avoiding mistakes.

Caution (a fancy word for waiting)

Is not imprinted on the wallpaper

Adorning the bedroom walls of Little Leaguers.

No. They dream beneath the images of action.

Unto itself good

(we have evolved from action and risk).

Yet, most often it is violence

Which is perceived as action

And packaged for profit

As a generic, nameless heroism

More deadly than nicotine

And far less satisfying.

(Sacrifice is a poor substitute for contribution.)

On what morning does a boy rise

To hear *what* man among us say

"Romance (a fancy word for trouble)

is the decisive action of a man *without* a plan?"

That passion is of the blood,

Yet, need not require the spilling of it?

Boys dream of being men;

But often they are prepped by myth

And schooled in a charade of manhood

Masquerading Death as if it were Life.

(Hypocrisy is the homage lie pays to truth).

Who said that? La Rochefoucauld?

To whom does a boy turn for counsel?

Who stands and declares himself as mentor?

Who speaks of brave compromise

And demonstrates the moral courage

Of negotiated settlement?

A *man* does.

And men *plan* for action

The Chinese say, "If you plan for a year, plant rice.

If you plan for ten years, plant trees

If you plan for one hundred years, grow men."

So, I ask you this Memorial Day,

What's the plan?

I do not ask *us*

I ask *you*. Personally.

This Memorial Day is different,

It is now. We are somewhat more

And somewhat less than before.

It is the nature of the universe to change,

It is the nature of humankind

To resist that change.

What we cannot do is deny it.

What we are supposed to do

Is to *create* some change of our own.

Become a part of a *positive* difference

Consider this:

Each man we knew who fell in combat

Remains as old as he will ever be

And each year we find another way to miss him, to remember

him,

And to grieve his loss.

We knew him when he was too young

To become all he was capable of being.

It is impossible to imagine

What books he might have read or written,

What children, what dreams,

He may have nurtured

Most were dead before they truly lived, few getting the chance to

dance

At his daughter's wedding

Or gloat over his son's first touchdown…

The men I remember

Were "lean and mean"

The men I remember

Never had a chance

To get fat, or go bald,

Lose teeth to bad gums

Or see Rambo get even.

The men I remember

Never had to pretend

"Slow-pitch" was real,

that macho was false,

or know John Lennon

was killed for nothing

(And nobody anywhere

gave "Peace a chance.")

So long as I breathe,

Each man I remember

Lives with me, in me

And I am responsible

To each for how I live…

Bob Foley

THE GROUP

Glenn A. Koch

I hate you, fear you, threaten to leave you
I plan and plot how I can deceive you.
And then I feel myself drawn back again,
And so I mingle in…
Edging into your circle of fellowship
As we feel each others Psychic pulse
I give my little cry for help.
It is disguised sometimes in laughter,
Trailing close behind some wall of words.
It is often soft and low and seemingly
With little interest, thought or feeling dropped
And then I pray, even in my fear
I pray against my outward wishes that you heard.
I pray to God you felt the tremor in the word.
And usually you do.
And with slow motions and ernest voice
You stab with deft precision where I hurt.
Sometimes you stab around the circle
And I marvel that I did not let the feeling show

With my emotions festered so.

I hurt, and I curse you for the moment then;

But when the poison's gone and pressure wanes,

I thank God that you were there

And that you heard and cared enough for me

To lance the inner boils and help to make me free.

At the end of group sessions, two sayings are recited,

the first to remind members of the need to deal with

the control issue and seek peace, the second as a

reminder of the need for a survivor's mission.

Grant us the serenity to accept the things we can't

change

Courage to change the things we can

And the wisdom to know the difference.

We owe it to those who didn't survive

to teach others what we know,

and to find some goodness,

some meaning to this life.

Bob Foley

From "Platoon"

About the Author

I have been a school counselor for twenty years, facilitating support groups and individual counseling for survivors of various traumas such as death of someone close including those who found the body, terminal illness, sex abuse, physical abuse and children of combat vets and chemical abusers. My experiences growing up in an alcoholic family and during Vietnam have helped me formulate a program that deals with the issues related to trauma: anger, guilt, loss, control, vulnerability and purpose.

www.ingramcontent.com/pod-product-compliance
Lightning Source LLC
Chambersburg PA
CBHW030345290526
45785CB00004B/1607